THE OFFICIAL HIBERNIAN FOOTBALL CLUB ANNUAL 2008

A Grange Publication

© 2007. Published by Grange Communications Ltd., Edinburgh, under licence from Hibernian Football Club. Printed in the EU.

Written by David Forsyth
Designed by Colin Heggie

Photographs © Action Images

ISBN 978-1-905426-84-3

£6.99

CONTENTS 2008

Welcome to the Hibernian Official 2008 Annual

INSIDE you will find profiles of the Squad, a chat with Club Captain Rob Jones, a profile of Hibernian Great Pat Stanton, a review of last season and, of course, a special feature on the CIS Cup victory.

We also enjoy an interview with the men charged with running Hibernian's famed Youth Academy, and readers can test their knowledge with our quizzes and brain teasers.

We hope you enjoy this year's edition and remember – Glory Glory to the Hibees! ■

CHAIRMAN'S
WELCOME

A FOOTBALL Club is about pride, passion and sporting achievement. It is also about families and communities identifying with, and supporting, their Club generation after generation.

It was one of our proudest days when the Club was able to reward our passionate and loyal supporters with a day of achievement and glory in March when the team won the CIS Insurance Cup – and in such thrilling and convincing style.

It was a just reward for a team which had provided so many with such entertainment. A team built by Tony Mowbray and then taken on by John Collins remained true to the Hibernian tradition of attacking, passing football.

The team included players developed though our own Hibernian Academy combined with players identified and brought to the Club by the Manager. This approach has served successive managers well and remains the focus of all of us involved at the Club. Our objective is always to put the best possible team out on the pitch.

To that end, another thrilling development has come to fruition this year with the opening of our state-of-the-art Training Centre in East Lothian. Both Tony Mowbray and John Collins identified this as the most important investment in football the Club could make, and at £4 million it certainly represents a significant investment.

The Training Centre, allied with the work being done within the Hibernian Academy structure, will ensure that this Club remains in the vanguard in the development of talented young players.

This balance of vital infrastructure improvements alongside continued financial commitment to the team allied with sensible financial management will ensure that the generations of Hibernian supporters to come can take pride in a competitive, vibrant and healthy Club. ■

SEASON REVIEW 06/07

JULY

THE SEASON kicked off in earnest right at the start of July, when Easter Road hosted Latvian side Dinaburg Daugavpils in the Inter Toto Cup, Hibernian clocking up an emphatic 5-0 win. The win was followed by the return leg, with Hibernian again winning convincingly, recording a 3-1 away win in Latvia. Two rounds then followed against Danish side Odense, skippered by former Hibernian favourite Ulrik Laursen. In the first leg, played in Denmark, Hibernian lost 1-0. In the return, a 2-1 home saw the side miss out, agonisingly, on goal difference. Interestingly, the match also pitted manager Tony Mowbray against his old Middlesboro' mentor, Bruce Rioch. A thrilling pre-season friendly against Premiership side Charlton ended in a 3-2 win for the Easter Road men, before the SPL action began at the end of July when Aberdeen came calling.

The game was a thriller, with Hibernian dominating and creating a series of chances but it was the Dons who took the lead against the run of play, with Dean Shiels snatching an equaliser for the Hibees. Those two first half goals proved to be the only scores of the day, the match ending 1-1, with Aberdeen relieved to have won a hard-fought point.

AUGUST

AUGUST began with an away fixture at Kilmarnock. Hibs opened the scoring when Shiels scored with a delightful chip, with the team flowing and creating chances. The second half proved different, with Killie on top and a Nish equaliser being followed by a solo effort from Naismith securing the points for the Ayrshire side. A long trip north to Inverness followed, with a scoreless draw gaining a scarce point for Hibernian in the Highlands, and then a 3-1 home win against Motherwell brought greater cheer. The month's SPL fixtures were rounded off with a visit to Parkhead to face Celtic.

Hibernian opened the scoring within the first ten minutes, a superb pass from Zemmama setting Scott Brown free and his low shot was enough to beat the keeper. With the home support getting increasingly nervy in the face of a stout defence and Hibs' slick counter-attacking threat a win looked on the cards until the hour mark, when Zurawski scored. The winner was nabbed by Jan Venegoor of Hesselink.

During August, Hibernian set off on their CIS Insurance Cup run, beating Peterhead 4-0 at Easter Road.

SEPTEMBER

A CONVINCING away win against Dundee United saw September off to a flying start, with three second half goals securing the points. Strikes from Killen, Shiels and Sproule went without reply. Rangers were next to call at Easter Road, the Ibrox men having had a mixed start to the season came expecting a difficult afternoon and were not disappointed as Hibs were at their fluent best and were unfortunate to win by a margin of only 2-1. Two headers from the in-form Killen either side of a Sebo goal for Rangers earning Hibernian a victory that had pundits purring over the quality of football on offer.

It was to prove a different story when Falkirk came calling, with four players being red-carded (two from each side) in a stormy, ill-tempered affair and an early strike from Milne sufficient to secure the Bairns the points. An away fixture at Love Street against St Mirren was the final match of the month, with Hibs again losing out 1-0.

A resounding 6-0 win at Easter Road against First Division leaders Gretna saw Hibs safely through the fourth round of the CIS Insurance Cup.

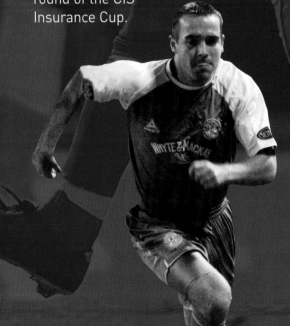

OCTOBER

OCTOBER was to be a month of high drama for Hibernian supporters, with the news unfolding that English giants West Bromwich Albion wanted Manager Tony Mowbray, and that he had agreed to join the Midlands side.

However on the pitch it had to be business as usual, and the month began with a high-octane derby at Easter Road. Hibs stormed into an early lead with strikes through Zemmama and Killen – two –up within 15 minutes. A goalkeeping error then allowed Hearts to score against the run of play, and thereafter the Tynecastle side fought their way back into contention and secured a draw when Velicka scored his second.

Another Hibernian first was notched on Monday, October 23rd, when the Club contested the first Monday night match to be screened live on Setanta, thrilling in a 4-0 demolition of Dunfermline at East End Park as Ivan Sproule ran amok. The month ended in Aberdeen with a 2-1 defeat, and the announcement of John Collins as the new Manager to succeed Tony Mowbray.

NOVEMBER

THE REIGN of John Collins as Hibernian Manager began at Easter Road with a home fixture against Kilmarnock, and it looked full of promise when an own goal from Hibs' defender Shelton Martis brought an enthralling response from the home side. Goals from Stewart and Fletcher looked to have secured the points until Naismith equalised.

Next up at Easter Road came Hearts, in the quarter final of the CIS Cup. A goal from Rob Jones, a crashing shot from within the box, was all Hibernian had to show on an afternoon in which they totally dominated their city rivals, but it was sufficient to march on to the semi finals.

A 2-0 home win against Inverness was followed by one of the performances of the season, a sizzling 6-1 demolition of Motherwell at Fir Park on an afternoon in which Hibs were, quite simply, unplayable. The month ended with an equally thrilling match against Celtic at Easter Road, Hibs taking a 2-0 lead with some scintillating football before being pegged back by a dogged Celtic who, even at this early stage, were showing the grit of champions.

DECEMBER

DUNDEE UNITED were first to come calling in December, with a visit to Easter Road ending with a 2-1 win to the home side, the goals coming from Jones and Fletcher after a freak own goal by Shelton Martis had put the Tannadice men ahead. A trip to Ibrox ended disappointingly in a 3-0 defeat, with the Rangers side inspired by Barry Ferguson emphatic winners. Another away trip, this time to Falkirk, also ended in a loss, by 2-1.

The brief losing streak was reversed in emphatic style just before Christmas, when St Mirren were hammered by 5 goals to 1 at Easter Road.

Boxing Day produced a thrilling derby encounter at Tynecastle, the Hearts side taking an early 2-0 lead before being pegged back to 2-2 through a Chris Killen strike and a Dean Shiels penalty. Unfortunately, Shiels was controversially sent off after tangling with Hearts keeper Craig Gordon in the penalty aftermath. Despite being a man down the Hibees looked as likely to score as their rivals, even after Mikolinius had hit what proved to be the winner. Indeed, Hibs were doubly unfortunate when a strike from Whittaker hit BOTH Hearts posts before staying out!

The month ended with a 2-0 home win against Dunfermline, two second half goals from Killen earning the points.

JANUARY

2007 began with a long trip to Pittodrie to face an Aberdeen side riding high in the league, but on a cold day there was little to cheer in a 0-0 draw.

The same opposition and venue awaited little more than a week later, in the third round of the Scottish Cup, and the match ended in a 2-2 draw, with Hibs more disappointed after being a goal up with just minutes to go. A league match away at Killie saw the manager rest several players, but the young team performed creditably and a 2-0 win was secured at a difficult venue.

The Cup replay at Easter Road was expected to produce another tight encounter, but Aberdeen were brushed aside as Hibs played fabulous football to earn a 4-1 win after going a goal behind.

That form couldn't be replicated in Inverness, with Hibernian again failing to produce in the Highland city and losing 3-0, but the month ended with a comfortable 2-0 league win against Motherwell at Easter Road.

The Club's CIS Cup march saw a vital obstacle overcome when a plucky and talented St Johnstone team took Hibs to extra time during the semi-final at Tynecastle. The 90 minutes ended all square at 1-1, but two extra time goals saw the Hibs on their way to Hampden.

January also saw the departure of skipper Kevin Thomson, in a £2 million move to Rangers.

FEBRUARY

FEBRUARY kicked off where January ended, with Cup success. Gretna provided the opposition at Easter Road in the fourth round of the Scottish Cup, and were determined to make amends for the 6-0 thrashing in the League Cup. A much better display saw a closer contest, but Hibs ran out 3-1 winners to go through to the quarter finals.

A visit to Parkhead followed, with Celtic running out 1-0 winners in another hard-fought and entertaining tussle, but the only winner when the team travelled to Tannadice to face Dundee United was an awful pitch. The match ended 0-0.

The Scottish Cup quarter final was a potential banana skin, with Hibs travelling to Dumfries to play Queen of the South. The match provide tricky and tense, with a David Murphy rocket opening the scoring for Hibernian. Queens then equalised, and a goal from substitute Thomas Sowumni was needed to secure progression to the semi final at Hampden.

MARCH

RANGERS visit to Easter Road at the start of the month proved to be disappointing, with two "soft" free kick goals by Charlie Adam earning Rangers the points. The following fixture provided a more satisfactory response, with Falkirk being overcome 2-0 at Easter Road.

The next game was the biggest of the season for the Hibees, the final of the CIS Insurance Cup, with a 5-1 win giving the Club its first trophy for 16 years.

The fans were out in force to back the team on a day that saw everything come to fruition in style.

19

APRIL

APRIL began in disappointing fashion, with a 1-0 defeat at home to Hearts. The game was marked by shirt-tugging and the high number of fouls, which prevented any free-flowing football.

A one-all draw away to St Mirren followed, with a Rob Jones goal being cancelled out by a late Saints equaliser through John Sutton. The team's poor away form continued at East End Park, where a Phil McGuire header consigned Hibs to another 1-0 loss, and the same opposition were faced a week later at Hampden in the Scottish Cup semi final. Despite dominating possession and territory, Hibernian were unable to find the net and the match ended 0-0, forcing a replay.

A young side took to the Pittodrie pitch to face an Aberdeen team going for third spot in the league and UEFA qualification. The youngsters surprised their more experienced opponents, twice going ahead before being pegged back in a 2-2 draw.

Next up was the most disappointing day of the season, the Scottish Cup Semi Final replay at Hampden, which saw Hibs go down 1-0 to a later penalty despite again dominating the match. The month ended with a thrilling 3-all draw against Rangers at Easter Road.

MAY

THE FINAL month of the season saw Kilmarnock first to visit Easter Road, desperate to avenge their Cup Final defeat. That they did so, by 1-0, was due almost entirely to the heroics of goalkeeper Alan Combe. His form on the day meant the Hibernian strikers could find no way past him.

A trip to Tynecastle produced another blank as Hearts struck twice early on to secure a 2-0 win, despite a second-half fight-back. The two early goals lost infuriated Manager John Collins, both being of the "very soft" variety.

The final match of the season was, fittingly, against Champions Celtic at Easter Road. In a pulsating match that belied its end-of-season status, Hibs ran out 2-1 winners after Celtic were put in front in the second half by Derek Riordan. The man scoring the equaliser was – most fittingly – Scott Brown, playing his last game for Hibs against his new employers. His heroic flying header was applauded by all four stands. Ivan Sproule then struck to secure the points. ∎

PLAYER QUIZ

1. Which two players were Club Captains during the season?

2. Name the Club's two Moroccan players

3. Which Hibs player spent time on loan at Dunfermline during the season?

4. Which country does Ivan Sproule represent?

5. Which player made his first-team debut against Aberdeen in the Cup in January?

6. From which Club did Hibernian sign David Murphy?

7. What nationality is Guillaume Beuzelin?

Answers on page 61

CUP WINNERS

SUNDAY, MARCH 18th was a day to rejoice for all Hibernian supporters as the 16-year wait for a trophy was brought to an end – and in what style!

Tens of thousands of green-and-white bedecked supporters crammed into Hampden to watch their heroes take on Kilmarnock as the teams running fifth and sixth in the league clashed in the final of the CIS Insurance Cup, a match many predicted could go all the way to extra time or even penalties.

"Too close to call" exclaimed the pundits and previewers, and indeed that tension was shared by many fans. The match, however, turned out very differently.

A 5-1 victory that was as stylish as it was emphatic was crowned with an emotional rendering of the Hibernian anthem, "Sunshine on Leith" following the presentation of the trophy.

Goals from Fletcher (2), Benjelloun (2) and Jones had put the fans into ecstasy, and the Killie fans could only look on as the celebrations began.

But it was entirely appropriate that the Final itself was won in such style by a team whose sparkling and entertaining play lit up not only the competition, but also the SPL campaign.

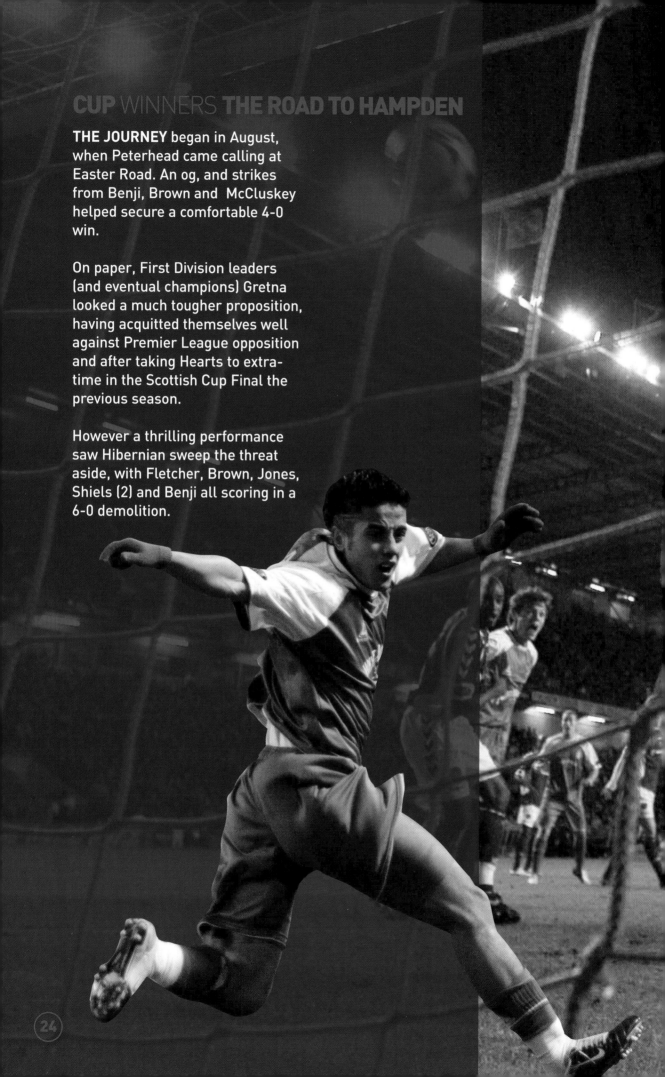

THE JOURNEY began in August, when Peterhead came calling at Easter Road. An og, and strikes from Benji, Brown and McCluskey helped secure a comfortable 4-0 win.

On paper, First Division leaders (and eventual champions) Gretna looked a much tougher proposition, having acquitted themselves well against Premier League opposition and after taking Hearts to extra-time in the Scottish Cup Final the previous season.

However a thrilling performance saw Hibernian sweep the threat aside, with Fletcher, Brown, Jones, Shiels (2) and Benji all scoring in a 6-0 demolition.

So far two rounds negotiated, ten goals scored and none conceded.

The Gretna win meant Hibs were through to the quarter finals, where the draw threw up the tie of the round – a derby clash against Hearts at Easter Road.

The game in November was only John Collins' second in charge following the departure of Tony Mowbray to West Brom and it saw the players turn in a sparkling performance. Hibernian were never in danger as they utterly dominated and outplayed the opposition, the only surprise being that the match only finished 1-0.

The semi-final now awaited, with St Johnstone providing the opposition having disposed of SPL sides – including Rangers – along the way. Tynecastle was the venue, and the ground was jammed to the rafters at the end of January when the sides met.

Saints could have felt unlucky to go behind during the regulation 90 minutes, and an equaliser was well-deserved to force the game to extra time. Superior fitness and technique finally came to the fore, and a David Murphy free kick settled the nerves before a Benji strike killed the match off.

The final, and the clash with Kilmarnock, awaited after four rounds with 14 goals scored and only one conceded.

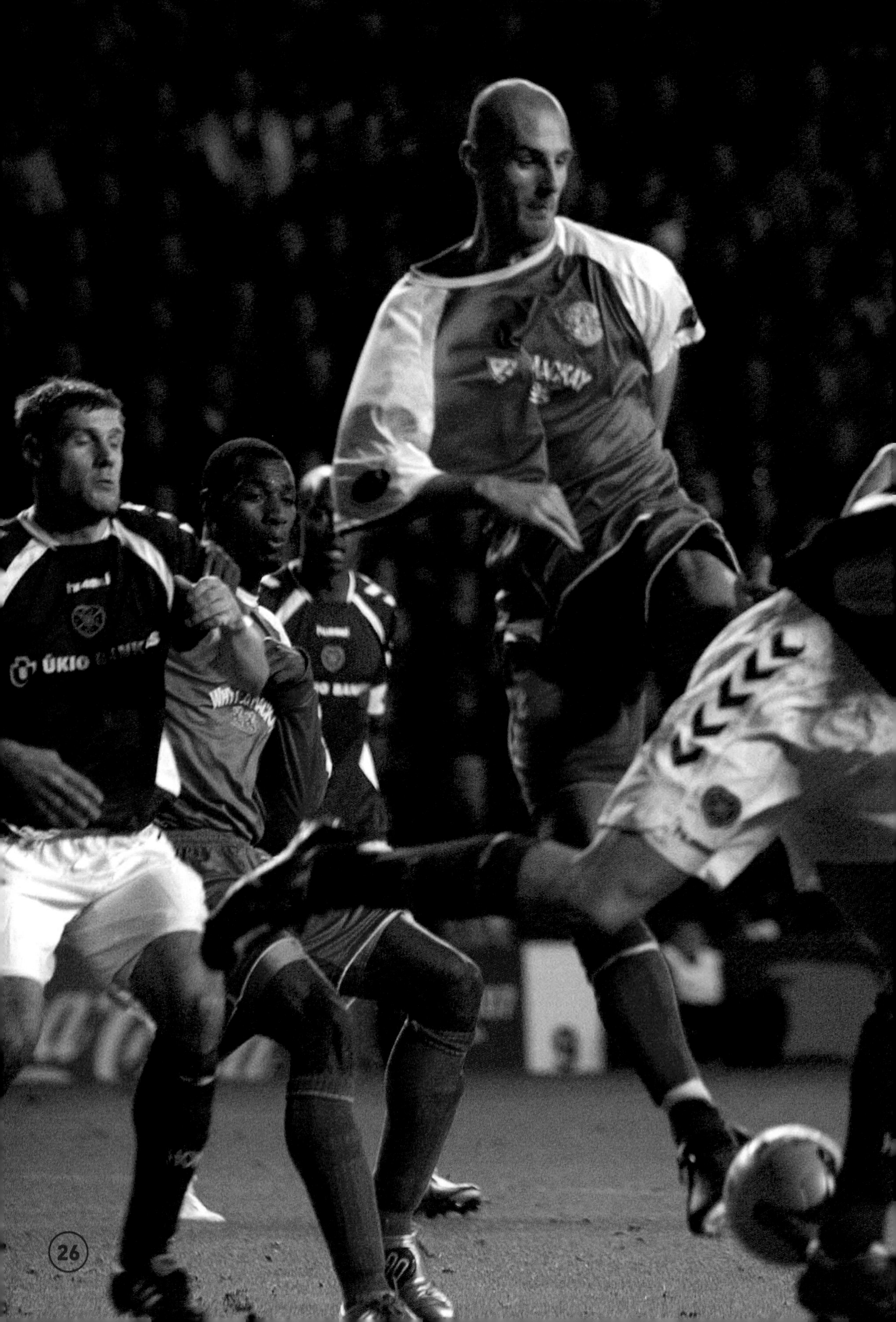

BOTH SETS of fans made the big day a special event, full of colour and song, with a real family feel.

Kilmarnock started the game well, with keeper Andy McNeil called on early to claw away an early strike on goal, his off balance save earning rapturous applause. Play raged from end to end, with Steven Naismith out jumping the Hibs keeper to get on the end of a long ball but the ball fell fortunately wide.

However it was Hibs who got the vital breakthrough after less than half an hour, skipper Rob Jones rising above everyone else to send a header into the net and send the Hibernian legions exultant.

That remained the score line at half time.

Benji unlocked the Killie defence into the second half with a twisting run and a rasping drive, and Fletcher then added a third to send Hibs 3-0 in front.

Killie continued to battle on, and when Greer scored a comeback appeared, briefly, to be a possibility before strikes from Benji and then Fletcher finally settled the nerves and ensured that the Cup would be decked out in green-and-white ribbons. In total, Hibernian had scored 19 goals in the Cup and conceded just two.

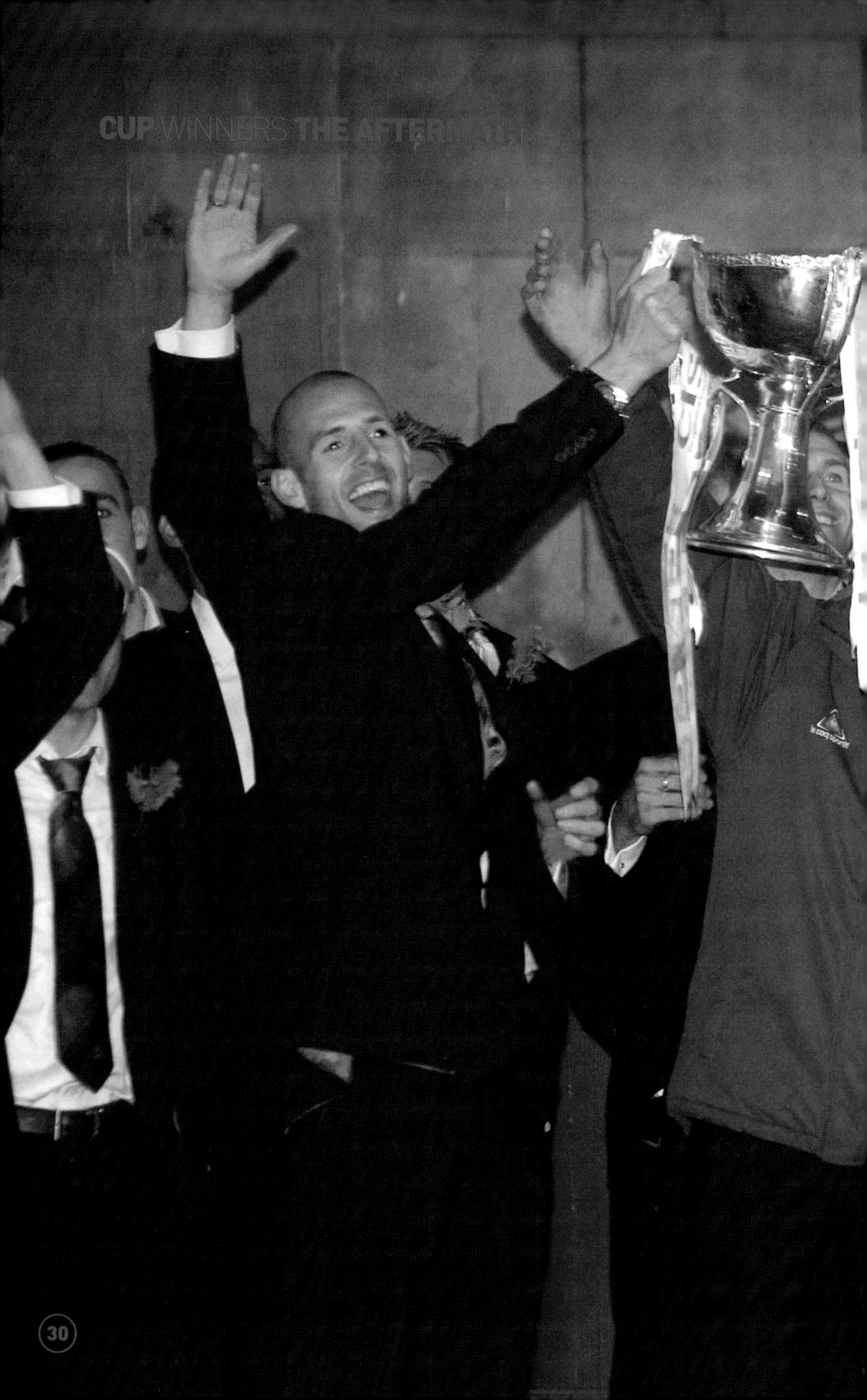

THE AFTER match celebrations were remarked on by commentators for the passionate rendition of "Sunshine on Leith" by the Hibs fans, and for the good natured celebrations which took place after skipper Rob Jones and Scott Brown lifted the cup together.

Then the team returned in happy mood to the City Chambers for a brief reception, followed by an open-top bus journey down the Mound, along Princes Street, down Leith Walk and up Easter Road to the Stadium where thousands more had gathered to greet the victorious heroes. ■

PAT STANTON
THE QUIET MAN

No former player is held in greater affection amongst the Hibernian support than Patrick Gordon Stanton.

THE MAN who led the Hibernian side that crushed Hearts 0-7 at Tynecastle on New Year's Day, 1973, has a place in the Club history alongside greats such as Joe Baker and – of course – the Famous Five.

His career is awash with highlights and great memories, including trophy wins, epic European encounters, and international honours.

Great, great, great grand nephew of the Club's first and original captain and one of its founders Michael Whelahan - the man credited with coming up with the Club's very name - Pat is woven into the fabric and history of the Club. It was entirely fitting that it was the Quiet Man who captained the Club in their centenary season.

A Craigmillar boy born and bred, Pat joined Hibernian from Bonnyrigg Rose Athletic. He had been a member of Holy Cross Academy's school team – the same side which had also provided his great friend Jimmy O'Rourke. But things could have turned out differently, as his potential had already been spotted by a rival manager with an eye for a player – one Jock Stein, then of Dunfermline.

The Pars boss who was to gain legendary status in the game had invited Pat to East End Park for a trial, but the youngster was by then also training with Hibs and was drawn to the green and white.

Hearts might also have been an option for Pat, but the influence of his Hibernian supporting family was too strong, his father telling him to sign on at Easter Road. Apart from the football, he was told, the strip was a lot better as well!

He was signed by Walter Galbraith in 1963, and went on to score on his debut in a 4-3 defeat to Motherwell. He was to go on to make almost 400 appearances, scoring 50 goals in the process, before a move to Celtic that saw him win further honours.

He enjoyed many highlights during his career, and has recounted many of them, including the night he played a friendly against mighty Real Madrid at Easter Road as an 18 year old in a Hibs team by then managed by Jock Stein:

"They were the biggest club in the world and it really upstaged Hearts (who were playing in Europe).

"It turned out to be a really magical night...That night even we stopped to watch along with the crowd as they came out of the tunnel. They looked like gods, all in white."

That night, Pat was designated to mark the world famous Puskas. The Hibs team had their own stars in Willie Hamilton, Neil Martin, Peter Cormack and Eric Stevenson and after surviving early pressure Hibernian grew to dominate the game and ran out 2-0 victors.

"They didn't like getting beaten that night and showed in some ways that they were just like any other players with a wee bit of bad temper here and there. Anyway, we won 2-0 and did a wee lap of honour afterwards."

Pat believes Stein's departure to Celtic was a crushing blow to Hibernian.

However Stein's friend Bob Shankly took over, and was in charge when another highlight was enjoyed, in 1967. Hibernian were playing in the UEFA Fairs Cup against Italian giants Napoli, and had lost 4-1 in Italy. They were given no chance in the return leg, but proved the sceptics wrong with a remarkable performance, winning 5-0 with Pat himself scoring the final goal.

"The night before the second leg the Napoli manager was so relaxed he was up in the directors' box with a large whisky watching them. He needed another large one after we were finished with them the next night."

It was also around this time, 1966, that Pat also won the first of his international caps. He was to go on to win 16, and prompted former Scotland manager Tommy Docherty to claim that he was

better than England's World Cup winning captain Bobby Moore at sweeper.

Pat became Hibernian captain in 1970, and a year later Eddie Turnbull – one of the Famous Five – arrived at the Club as Manager.

In 1972, Turnbulls Tornadoes won the League Cup, defeating Celtic 2-1 in the Final through goals from Stanton and O'Rourke. Celtic's scorer that day was Kenny Dalglish. "We could have won by a greater margin, but to hear the final whistle and realise we had won the Cup was a terrific feeling."

A year later, and one of the major highlights of his career arrived as a welcome first foot on January 1st 1973.

"The thing about the 7-0 game was that we could all feel something like that was coming. We had just won the League Cup, beaten Ayr 8-1 and run up big scores against Sporting Lisbon and K Besa.

"Hearts could actually have been a goal or two up before we scored, but then again we could have got ten that day. At half time Eddie Turnbull told us to keep going and not let up. But I suppose we did a bit, although we were always creating chances."

Pat's playing career at Easter Road came to an end a few years later, in 1976, when he was sold to Jock Stein's Celtic in a deal which saw Jackie McNamara head east. Pat won a League and Cup double in his first season in Glasgow, but an injury saw his career end in 1977.

He returned to Easter Road as Manager in 1982, replacing Bertie Auld, and served in that position for two years. ∎

PAT STANTON
FACTFILE

Patrick Gordon Stanton

Date of Birth September 13th, 1944 in Edinburgh

Joined Hibernian in 1963 from Bonnyrigg Rose

European Victories included CF Barcelona, Liverpool,
Real Madrid, Sporting Lisbon

1972 League Cup winning captain

398 appearances for Hibs,

50 goals

16 Scotland Caps

NEW FACES

TORBEN JONELEIT joined the Club in time for pre-season training. Torben had agreed a new three-year deal with his club, AS Monaco, but was keen to spend the first year on loan at Hibernian.

Torben (20) is German and has honours at Under-21 level for his country.

On signing him, Hibernian Manager John Collins said: "Torben is an exceptionally talented defender who has so far had limited first-team opportunities at Monaco. He is very highly rated by his club who have only recently signed him on a three-year contract and we are delighted that they have agreed to allow him to add to his experience by playing for Hibernian for the next year.

"He is a strong defender who is comfortable with both feet and I am convinced he will prove to be an asset to the football club this season."

The player himself made reference to the attraction of joining a Club managed by John Collins, himself a renowned Monaco player.

GIANT goalkeeper Yves Makabu-Ma-Kalambay signed for Hibernian from Chelsea on 1 July.

Yves was the first choice of Manager John Collins to strengthen the all important goalkeeping department. The player agreed a three year deal.

Yves was born in Brussels on January 31st 1986 to parents from the Democratic Republic of Congo; he has played at Under-21 international level for Belgium. After starting his career at PSV Eindhoven, Yves was snapped up by Chelsea on 1st July 2003.

During his four seasons with Chelsea he has been understudy to Petr Cech, Carlo Cudicini and latterly Henrique Hilario.

John Collins said of him: "He has tremendous potential, he is a good height for a goalkeeper at 6' 5" tall, is very strong and athletic, in fact he has all the attributes you could expect to find in a player in that position.

"He has benefited from world-class coaching at Chelsea under Silvino Lauro but such is the quality of goalkeepers at Chelsea there was little opportunity for first-team football and at this stage in his career that is what Yves is seeking."

CLUB QUIZ

1. When was Hibernian Founded?

2. How many times has the Club won the League Cup?

3. What was the name of the Club's most famous forward line?

4. Who was the first Captain of Hibernian?

5. Who was Manager when Hibs defeated Hearts 7-0 on New Year's Day,1973?

6. From which Club did Jock Stein join as Manager?

7. Which Italian Club did Hibs defeat 5-0 at Easter Road in the Fairs Cup?

8. Who scored a hat-trick against Hearts in the 6-2 win at Easter Road in season 2000-01?

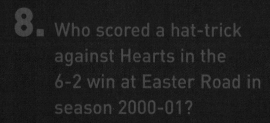

Answers on page 61

PLAYER **PROFILES**

GOALKEEPERS:

ANDY McNEIL joined Hibernian from Southampton in January 2006. The 20-year-old was delighted to come to Easter Road after growing up as a fan of the Club. Under John Collins the Scotland u-20 internationalist has quickly established himself in the first team squad, playing a vital role in the CIS Insurance Cup win with a brilliant one-handed save early in the first half. Agile and quick, he is a young man with a big future in the game.

DEFENDERS:

DAVID MURPHY provides the perfect balance on the left flank. The 23-year-old left back is a product of Middlesbrough's renowned Academy before joining Hibernian, and he has now made more than 100 appearances for the Club. Like Whittaker, he enjoys surging forward and his powerful left foot has secured a number of vital goals for the Club. David is also renowned for his consistency, and for his deft first touch.

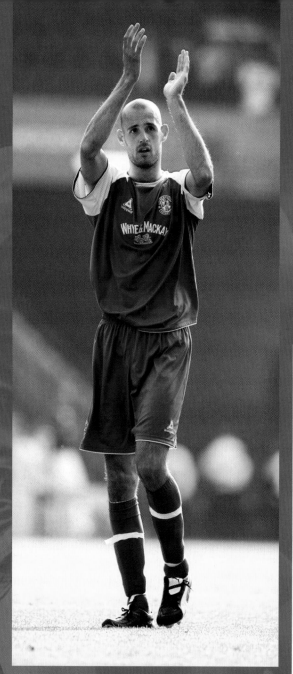

CHRIS HOGG is a player in a hurry. After an injury blighted start to his career at Easter Road Chris (22) really found his feet at Hibernian in the second half of last season. The former England youth captain joined the Club from Ipswich Town, and his pace, courage and aerial ability saw him enjoy the best form of his Hibernian career to date – form he is determined to build on in the season ahead.

ROB JONES is the Club Captain, and is very much the team's leader on the pitch. The 6ft 7in centre back came to the Club in the summer of 2006 in a £100,000 move from English Championship side Grimsby. As well as his defensive qualities, Rob (28) provides a goal threat for opposition sides and popped up with a stunning nine goals during last season. Two for which he will be lauded for a long time are a stunning close-range shot that secured a 1-0 win against arch-rivals Hearts in the CIS Cup quarter final at Easter Road, and his opening goal – a trademark towering header – in the final itself.

DERMOT McCAFFREY made one appearance last season, against Aberdeen in a hard-fought draw when Hibernian fielded a young side that showed the future of the Club is in capable hands.

KEVIN McCANN made his breakthrough into the first team in a match at Aberdeen last season, turning in a performance that brought praise from manager John Collins and media alike. Since then, the 20-year-old product of the Hibernian youth system has gone on to produce several outstanding displays, including a fine long-range strike against Rangers. A right back, Kevin has also turned in excellent displays in midfield that augur well for the Club's future.

DEFENDER/MIDFIELDER

LEWIS STEVENSON has proven to be a real rising star during last season. The 19-year-old is yet another product of the Hibernian Academy, and is developing into a high-quality and flexible left-sided player. Lewis' form was such that he started the CIS Insurance Cup Final, turning in a polished display that won him the Man of the Match award. Although mainly a left-back, he has been operating mainly on the left side of midfield for the Club. He is an outstanding prospect.

MIDFIELD

MEROUANE ZEMMAMA is the kind of exciting player fans pay to watch. The Moroccan ace joined the Club at the start of last season, but his debut was delayed while international paperwork was completed. Talented, stylish and confident the midfielder is a box of attacking tricks who has a key role to play at the Club. Injury and delays have limited his appearances to just 17, but much more looks likely in future from this 24-year-old playmaker.

GUILLAUME BEUZELIN is one of the mainstays of the side. The stylish central midfielder has an unerring eye for the pass and his stylish contribution also belies a steel core that brings essential bite and combative qualities to the midfield area. The 28-year-old Frenchman is a firm fans' favourite. "Boozy" has already made more than 70 appearances for the Club.

DEAN SHIELS came through the Arsenal Academy before joining Hibernian in the summer of 2004. An intelligent, hard-working player with an eye for goal, Dean is one of the current squad who has the distinction of scoring a winning goal against Hearts. He fought back from eye surgery in a way that gained praise from all corners of the game in Scotland, and his clever running and ability to finish has won many admirers for the 22-year-old.

THIERRY GATHEUSSI Cameroon international defender Thierry Gatheussi signed for the Club in July.

The 25-year-old signed a two-year deal after impressing at the club's pre-season training camp in Austria, and after he continued to impress on returning to Easter Road for a further week.

Manager John Collins said of him "Thierry is an accomplished player who can play on either the left or right side of defence and has in fact played in central defence at his previous clubs, and so gives us a few more options in that area. We are delighted to have him at the club."

Gatheussi was born in Bafoussam, Cameroon on 17th April 1982. He joined Hibernian from French side FC Sete having started his career at Montpellier for whom he made 49 appearances. He had one international appearance for Cameroon against Bulgaria in April 2004 before moving on in 2005 to Cannes. After 27 appearances Thierry joined FC Sete a year later, making 29 appearances in his first season with the second division side.

ROSS CHISHOLM is another product of the Hibernian Academy who comes firmly into the "one to watch" category. The central midfielder made a number of appearances towards the end of last season, impressing with his mature displays and his ability to play box to box, tackling and passing. Has the potential to become a complete midfielder.

BRIAN KERR'S move to Easter Road saw the midfielder joining forces once again with Assistant Manager Tommy Craig, with whom he worked at Newcastle United. Brian (25) is a passing midfielder, who has won three full Scotland caps during his career. He joined the Club from Motherwell in the summer.

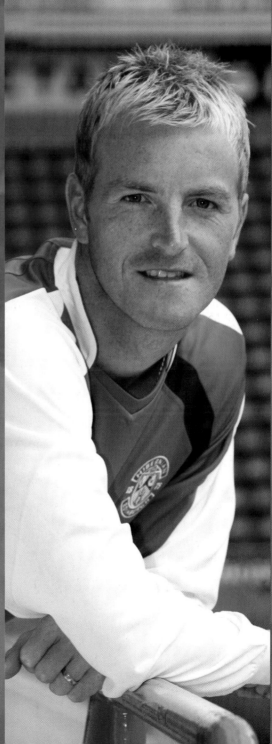

SEAN LYNCH is a hard-working midfielder who made a handful of starts for Hibernian last season. A product of the Club's own Academy, he has broken through to the fringes of the first team and is an increasingly important member of the first-team squad. Tough in the tackle, he is a young man with a solid future ahead and gained recognition through selection for the Scotland under 20 squad.

FILIPE MORAIS signed for the club from Milwall during the summer on a two-year contract. The 21-year-old started his senior career at Chelsea before moving on to Milwall a year ago. A right-sided midfielder, he spent some time on loan to St Johnstone last season, playing against Hibernian in the CIS Insurance Cup Semi-Final at Tynecastle. He made 13 appearances for the Saints scoring once.

John Collins said: " He is very strong while comfortable on the ball, I would say he is exactly the type of player we are looking for at Hibernian."

STRIKERS

ABDESSALAM BENJELLOUN, or Benji as he is known with great affection by Hibernian fans, has shown continuous improvement since joining the Club. The talented striker (aged 22) has shown an increasing appetite for the physical nature of the game in Scotland, and his strength allied to his technical ability makes him a difficult opponent whose reputation continues to grow.

STEVEN FLETCHER continues to develop and impress at both Club and international level, where he has led the line for Scotland at a variety of age group levels including under 20. The 20-year-old has a sweet left foot, pace and mobility, and the courage to go in where it hurts allied with a formidable work-rate. Another product of the Hibernian Academy system, Steven is a player with a very big future.

CLAYTON DONALDSON (23) was Manager John Collins' first signing, joining the Club this summer from Conference side York City. The 6ft 2 in striker has pace and strength in abundance and will be hoping that his excellent goal-scoring ratio in the Conference can be translated to the SPL.

DAMON GRAY made a dream debut at Aberdeen towards the end of last season, scoring in his first match for the first team. The young Geordie-born striker then continued the dream by starting the Scottish Cup semi final at Hampden. One for the future. ◼

ROSS CAMPBELL made two appearances for the Club last season, the youngster forcing his way through the ranks from under 19 level. Quick, clever and a natural finisher he has also achieved international recognition at age group levels, travelling with the under 20 squad to Canada in the summer.

A LOOK AT OUR HISTORY

HIBERNIAN Football Club, founded in 1875 by the Irish immigrant community in Edinburgh, was the first British club to enter European competition in 1955. That year Hibs went on to reach the semi-finals only to be defeated by a Reims side inspired by great French footballer Raymond Kopa.

This period was Hibernian's most successful when they had the forward line known as "The Famous Five" made up of Gordon Smith, Bobby Johnstone, Lawrie Reilly, Eddie Turnbull and Willie Ormond.

Hibs had won the League championship in 1947/48, 1950/51, and 1951/52, and were famed for their attacking football.

Hibernian reached the semi-finals of the Fairs Cup (UEFA) in 1961 before losing to Roma in a third match play-off in the Olympic Stadium.

Over the next decade Hibs played host to clubs such as Juventus, Porto, Leeds United and Liverpool in UEFA competition. In 1968 they beat Napoli 5-0. The Italians' goalkeeper that night was none other than Dino Zoff.

On the home front Hibs, managed by Eddie Turnbull, again achieved success winning the League Cup in 1972,

defeating Jock Stein's Celtic team. During that period they picked up the Drybrough Cup twice in 1972 and 1973.

For a decade, from 1979 to 1989 Hibs missed out on European competition, only returning in 1989 under the leadership of Alex Miller, who managed Hibernian through a difficult period in the club's history.

In 1990, Wallace Mercer of city rivals Heart of Midlothian staged a controversial attempt to take-over the Club and close it down leaving only one senior club in Edinburgh. Sir Tom Farmer CBE saved the Club in 1991.

After two years of turmoil, the new stability brought to the Club paid immediate dividends to the fans when Hibs won the 1991 Skol League Cup. In 1996, after ten years at Easter Road, Alex Miller left Hibs and, after a brief spell with Jocky Scott in charge, Hibs appointed Jim Duffy as their Manager. After a downturn in fortunes on the field Duffy's short spell as manager was ended in February 1998 and he was replaced by former Scotland internationalist Alex McLeish. Alex's late arrival in the season was not enough to stop Hibs finishing bottom of the Premier league and being relegated for only the third time in their history.

and he was to be replaced by Bobby Williamson, who joined from Kilmarnock.

Tony Mowbray arrived at the club to take over from Bobby Williamson who had departed at the end of the 2004/05 season to Plymouth. From that May 24th 2004 arrival, Tony promised to have Hibernian playing the type of free-flowing, attacking football that he knew the traditions of Hibernian Football Club demanded.

He had the difficult task of taking Hibernian into the First Division and straight back up again. However Hibs went on to enjoy a record-breaking season, which saw the team crowned worthy Champions of the Scottish Football League.

The 2004/05 season was one of the most exciting seen at Easter Road since the 1970s. Hibernian finished the season in 3rd place, and in doing so they were back in Europe - fittingly given that this was the 50th anniversary year of Hibernian making that very first British entry into the European Cup.

In season 2000/2001, they blasted through the early season, recording six consecutive victories in August, and an unbeaten Hibs side sat proudly at the top of the SPL table, finally finishing third. Hibs also reached the final of the Tennent's Scottish Cup for the first time in 22 years but lost to Celtic at Hampden Park.

The following season the attacking football continued and the Club achieved fourth place in the league and got to the semi final of the Scottish Cup.

A brand new West Stand was completed for the start of season 2001/2002. Hibs also enjoyed European football and the Easter Road Club did themselves proud by almost knocking AEK Athens out of the UEFA Cup. Hibs lost 2-0 in Athens but recorded a 3-2 win at Easter Road (after extra-time).

Last season was underway when West Brom came calling for Mowbray, who was replaced by former Easter Road hero John Collins, and he was at the helm when the team claimed silverware for the first time in 16 years with a thrilling 5-1 demolition of Kilmarnock in the CIS Insurance League Cup Final at Hampden in March 2007. ■

Alex McLeish and Andy Watson departed for Ibrox and fans' favourite Franck Sauzee was installed as new Club manager. However the results didn't happen under the popular Frenchman

CLUB HONOURS

FOUNDED:	1875	
Scottish League Winners	(4)	1902/03, 1947/48, 1950/51, 1951/52
First Division winners	**(2)**	**1980/81, 1998/99**
Division Two winners	(3)	1893/94, 1894/95, 1932/33
Division One runners-up	**(6)**	**1896/97, 1946/47, 1949/50, 1952/53, 1973/74, 1974/75**
Scottish Cup winners	(2)	1887, 1902
Scottish Cup runners-up	**(9)**	**1896, 1914, 1923, 1924, 1947, 1958, 1972, 1979, 2001**
Scottish League Cup winners	(3)	1972/73, 1991/92, 2006/07
Scottish League Cup runners-up	**(6)**	**1950/51, 1968/69, 1974/75, 1985/86, 1993/94, 2003/04**
Drybrough Cup winners	(2)	1972/73, 1973/74
Summer Cup winners	**(2)**	**1941, 1964**
Tennents Sixes winners	(1)	1989/90
BP Youth Cup winners	**(1)**	**1991/92**
European Cup		six matches (best: semi-final 1955/56)
Cup Winners' Cup		**six matches (best: third round 1972/73)**
UEFA/Fairs Cup		60 matches (best: semi-final Fairs Cup 1960/61)
Record Home Attendance		**65,860 versus Heart of Midlothian, January 2 1950**
Most Capped Player		Lawrie Reilly, 38, Scotland
Most League Appearances		**Arthur Duncan, 446**
Most League goals scored in a season by an individual		Joe Baker, 42, 1959/60 season
Most goals scored by an individual (all seasons)		**Gordon Smith, 364**

LEAGUE TABLES AND SCORERS

	P	W	D	L	Pts
Celtic	38	26	6	6	84
Rangers	38	21	9	8	72
Aberdeen	38	19	8	11	65
Hearts	38	17	10	11	61
Kilmarnock	38	16	7	15	55
Hibernian	**38**	**13**	**10**	**15**	**49**
Falkirk	38	15	5	18	50
Inverness	38	11	13	14	46
Dundee Utd	38	10	12	16	42
Motherwell	38	10	8	20	38
St Mirren	38	8	12	18	36
Dunfermline	38	8	8	22	3

TOP SCORERS

Chris Killen	15	**Rob Jones**	09
Benji	14	**Dean Shiels**	09
Steven Fletcher	11	**Scott Brown**	08
Ivan Sproule	10	**David Murphy**	03

WEARING THE
ARMBAND

When John Collins looked around the dressing room to select a skipper to lead his young side one figure stood tall – in every way.

BIG Rob Jones, all 6ft 7ins of him, was the choice of the Manager and what a season it turned out to be for the skipper culminating in lifting the Club's first silverware at a packed and emotional Hampden Park in March.

It's no surprise that March 18th, 2007 is a special date for the big centre half who's rapidly established himself as a favourite with the fans for his heart-on-his-sleeve attitude and his 100% commitment.

He said: "First and foremost to be the captain of this Club is such an honour, and one I did not expect to happen to me. To go up the stairs at Hampden and lift the Cup was just amazing. To see and hear what it meant to all of those fans – fantastic.

"And then to be on the open top bus and to see all of those tens of thousands of fans out in the streets celebrating, dancing and singing, it really took my breath away. I couldn't believe it."

Being captain has been a learning curve for the big man, as he himself admits: "You learn something new about yourself every day, and with the responsibility of being captain you have to learn, and learn fast.

52

"But it's a role I relish, and we have a great bunch of lads here so I am looking forward to the season ahead. We've won a trophy, so we've got a taste for more and I'd like to be a part of a successful era at this Club."

The former school-teacher is also a popular figure with the press, giving articulate and honest interviews. It's a side of the captaincy he has also had to grow accustomed to. "When you are the captain, there are times when you have to stand up and be counted – for example following the derby defeat at Easter Road. You may not enjoy it, but it goes with the territory."

He confesses the captaincy matters greatly to him. "It would hurt to have it removed from me, it means a lot to me. A year and a bit ago I was playing at Grimsby and before that I was teaching primary school children, so to even be at a Club like Hibernian is fantastic, never mind to be captain of the Club."

But he is determined he will be a successful captain, leading a successful team: "At times, we've shown just how good we are and how good we can become. The 5-1 defeat of Killie in the CIS Cup Final in March was unbelievable as no one could ever have envisaged winning a cup final in that manner.

"We played well in other games last season, including the 2-1 victory over Rangers at Easter Road, but we must strive to find greater consistency. The young players are becoming older, wiser and even fitter and that has to show in better results and more trophies. I hope so." ∎

STADIUM QUIZ

1. When was the stadium inaugurated?

2. What is the capacity?

3. When, and against whom, was the attendance record set?

4. What Italian ground is the stadium nick-named for by Hibs fans?

5. Which pop star played in concert at the stadium in 2005?

6. What Scottish artiste was the support act?

7. Which two nations clashed in a thrilling World Cup warm up in 2006?

8. After which Hibernian forward line is the North Stand named?

9. Which stand houses the main reception?

10. What famous Easter Road characteristic disappeared in season 1999/2000?

Answers on page 61

NEW FACES

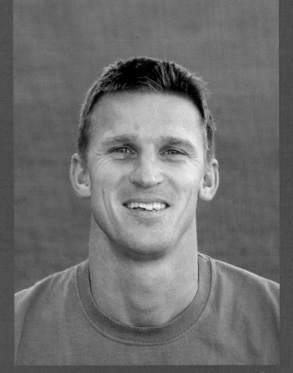

FLYING winger Alan O'Brien also joined Hibernian during the summer after spending six seasons with Newcastle United.

He was at United from age 16 where he progressed under the guidance of a number of coaches, including Hibernian's Assistant Manager Tommy Craig. He has made 5 English Premiership and FA Cup appearances for Newcastle and one in the UEFA Intertoto Cup last season. He also made 5 appearances while on loan to Carlisle in a spell that saw him score his first senior goal on his debut appearance against Bristol Rovers.

He has represented his country at Under-14's, 15's, 16's, 19's and finally at full international level, making his debut for the Republic of Ireland against Holland in his native Dublin in August 2006. He went on to appear last season against Germany, Cyprus and the Czech Republic in European Championship Qualifying games.

Alan said: "Everybody in the game is I think aware of what has been happening at Hibernian over the last few years, the quality of young players coming through the ranks into first-team football is exceptional. I enjoyed my time at Newcastle United immensely but I believe that with Hibernian I can progress both at Club and International level."

A FORMER favourite of Hibernian Football Club returned to the fold in the summer when former player Gareth Evans was appointed as Reserve Team Coach.

Gareth expressed his delight thus: "I was delighted to join the Club. It's great to be back at Easter Road. A lot has changed since I played for the Club, but I am looking forward to helping to take things forward. "

Gareth (40) played for Hibernian between 1988 and 1996 having previously played for Coventry City and Rotherham United. He also had spells with Partick Thistle and Airdrie. Gareth began coaching in 2000 and was Assistant Manager at Alloa Athletic and at Brechin City.

Gareth took up his post on 16 July 2007 with responsiblity for training reserve team players and coaching Hibernian's team which participates in the SPL Reserve League. The role was previously undertaken by Mark Proctor who left to take up the position as Manager of Livingston FC. ∎

ACADEMY NEWS

A new team heads up Hibernian's vaunted Academy – with the appointment in the summer of Bill Hendry as Academy Manager and Alastair Stevenson as Academy Coach.

THE DUO will be responsible for a youth development system that is the envy of the country, having produced a real crop of talented young players in recent years – many of them going on to claim full international honours such as Scott Brown, Derek Riordan and Gary O'Connor.

In addition, the Club supplied a significant core of players – four in total – for Scotland's under 20 side which competed in Canada during the summer, and we also enjoy representation at international level throughout the age groups.

Young stars who broke through last season included Lewis Stevenson – who turned in an eye-catching Man of the Match performance in the CIS Insurance Cup final, Kevin McCann, Ross Chisholm, Sean Lynch, Dermot McCaffrey and Ross Campbell.

The good news is that the conveyor belt looks set to rumble on. Bill Hendry said: "Take my word for it, we have good players at every age group and some really exceptional ones. That's what we always strive for, to bring through players who have a real chance of making it all the way to the first team."

Alastair added: "If you can bring through one or two players each season then you are doing really well, but that continual flow of talent is our objective. And we have some really exciting prospects coming through." ∎

ONE TO WATCH
THIS SEASON

Kevin McCann is walking proof of the Hibernian Academy determination to produce talented, rounded footballers.

THE 20-YEAR-OLD, who made his debut last season, plays most of his football at right back but can also operate in midfield – a position from which he scored a stunning goal against Rangers last term.

His showings earned him high praise from John Collins, who described him thus: "He's strong, very focused and good on the ball."

Kevin himself admits his delight at being involved in first team action, and his desire to earn more starting slots this season. He said: "It has been a great experience, testing myself at this level. I enjoy it, and the aim has to go on to become a first-pick and then push on from there."

Kevin has been with the Club for around nine years, first training with the Club through its training camps in the West and then coming through to join up at Easter Road at 16 years old.

"You could say I've served a long apprenticeship but hopefully I'm going to be around for a number of years to come during which we'll go on to win things. It was amazing coming on in the Cup Final, and to be a part of a winning squad was just amazing. I'm lucky to have got that experience so early in my career. Now I want more." ∎

NEW FACES

CLAYTON DONALDSON (23) was John Collins' first signing, the 6ft 2in striker arriving at Easter Road in the summer from York City.

Pacy and direct, the striker's only regret was that his previous Club failed to win through in their play-offs from the conference. Other than that, his only emotion was one of happiness.

"I'm very impressed with the set up here at Easter Road. It's a big step up for me, and a challenge I am enjoying. There are lots of good players and lots of competition for places – just like it should be at a big club like this."

Clayton is determined to make the most of the opportunity that has presented itself. "I've shown people that I can play at a higher level than the Conference. I have faith in my ability – lots of good players have come from lower leagues over the years."

BRIAN KERR'S move to Easter Road saw a reunion –the midfielder joining forces once again with Assistant Manager Tommy Craig.

Kerr (25) worked with Tommy at Newcastle United, and rates the coach highly. "I was desperate to work with Tommy again as I loved my time under him at Newcastle."

He believes the move from Motherwell could help resurrect his international career, the last of his 3 caps being achieved some time ago. "I believe Tommy and John Collins, as midfielders themselves, are two people who can enhance my game and my career. They were big factors in me joining."

He was also attracted by the philosophy of passing, attacking football espoused at Hibernian – an ethos he believes suits his own strengths. "I get more leeway to get forward and that allows me to express myself more as a player.

"I am delighted to be here. I just hope this is the start of an era which brings success to Hibs – that's what we all want to achieve." ■

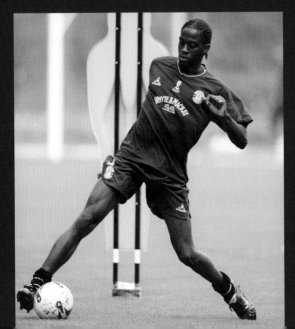

CLUB CONTACTS

CLUB ADDRESS
Hibernian Football Club
Easter Road Stadium
12 Albion Place
Edinburgh
EH7 5QG
Telephone: 0131 661 2159
Ticket Box Office: 0844 844 1875

MATCH-DAY HOSPITALITY & ADVERTISING
Amanda Vettese
Corporate Hospitality Manager
avettese@hibernianfc.co.uk
Tel: 0131 656 7073

Russell Smith
Commercial Manager
rsmith@hibernianfc.co.uk
Tel: 0131 656 7072

GENERAL E-MAIL
club@hibernianfc.co.uk

GENERAL ENQUIRIES
club@hibernianfc.co.uk
Tel: 0131 661 2159

TICKET OPERATIONS
Judith Quinn
Ticket Office Manager
jquinn@hibernianfc.co.uk
Tel: 0844 844 1875

QUIZ ANSWERS

PLAYERS QUIZ

1. Kevin Thomson, Rob Jones
2. Zemmama, Benjí
3. Stephen Glass
4. Northern Ireland
5. Kevin McCann
6. Middlesboro'
7. French

CLUB QUIZ

1. 1875
2. three times
3. Famous Five
4. Michael Whelahan
5. Eddie Turnbull
6. Dunfermline
7. Napoli
8. Mixu Paatelainen

STADIUM QUIZ

1. 1893
2. 17,500
3. Hearts in 1950 (65,860)
4. San Siro
5. Elton John
6. Lulu
7. South Korea and Ghana
8. Famous Five
9. West Stand
10. The Slope